BOOK OF

CLEAN JOKES

Dan Harmon

BARBOUR
PUBLISHING

Published by Barbour Publishing, Inc., P.O. Box 719, Uhrichsville, Ohio 44683, www.barbourbooks.com

Our mission is to publish and distribute inspirational products offering exceptional value and biblical encouragement to the masses.

ecpa Member of the
Evangelical Christian
Publishers Association

Printed in the United States of America.
5 4 3 2 1

Contents

AGE

Two children were caught
in mischief by their grandmother.
Happily, she chose not to punish them. "Remember," she
mused, "I used to be young once, too."

"Gee, Gram," said one of the children, wide-eyed. "You
sure have an incredible memory!"

"What causes old age, Grandpa?"
"Living."

The grandparents listened respectfully as little Sherman
described what he'd learned in history class. "We saw a
video of the first man landing on the moon! His name was
Neil Armstrong."

Grandpa turned to Grandma. *"History?* I thought that
was current events."

A ninety-five-year-old gentleman entered a life insurance
office and told the agent he wanted to take out a three-
hundred-thousand-dollar whole-life policy.

"But you're simply too old," the agent said after a
moment's consideration. "No insurance company would
start a new policy on a ninety-five-year-old client."

"Sonny boy," the applicant steamed, "are you aware of the mortality demographics within the United States of America?"

"Why, yes, Sir. I believe I know the statistics pretty well."

"What percentage of the population is known to die between the ages of 90 and 120?"

"Er, something less than 5 percent. . . ."

"Then what, exactly, is your problem with my age bracket?"

The agent wrote the policy.

"Dad, what's middle age?"

"That's when you lose all your growth at the top and do all your growing in the middle."

A widow was describing to a friend the gentleman she'd recently been dating.

"Does he wear his hair parted or unparted?" her friend asked.

"Actually. . .departed."

An elderly man took his faithful but weather-beaten Packard to a tune-up shop for an oil change. The two mechanics exchanged glances as the car puttered to a stop at the garage door.

"Man," said one with a low whistle, "I'll bet that thing's still insured against Indian attack."

AIRPLANES

The transatlantic flight to England was halfway across when the pilot came on the intercom with a casual message to the passengers. "You may have noticed a slight change in the sound of the engines. That's because we've had to shut down Engine 2 temporarily. There's no cause for concern; we have three more engines in fine condition. But there'll be a slight delay. Our expected time of arrival has been changed from 2:14 P.M. to 2:45 P.M. Sorry for any inconvenience this may cause."

An hour later the pilot was back on the intercom, chuckling softly. "Folks, this is the first time I've ever experienced this, and I never thought it would happen, but we seem to have lost power in Engine 4. No problem in terms of safety, but we'll have a further delay. We now expect to arrive at Heathrow International at 3:30 P.M."

And a little while later he was back at the mike, still trying to sound reassuring but with an edge in his voice. "You won't believe this, but Engine 1 seems to be on the blink, and we've decided it's wise to shut it down. This is a weird situation, but not really alarming. We can easily finish the flight with one engine, although we'll be flying substantially slower. We now anticipate arriving around 4:25 P.M."

One passenger turned to another and mumbled, "If that last engine goes out, it'll be next Tuesday till we get to England."

The first-time flier was not assured when the flight attendant cheerily pointed out that the passenger seat could be removed and used as a flotation device. "I'd much rather be sitting on a parachute," he remarked to the person next to him.

A man edged his way down the aisle to what he thought was his row aboard a jetliner awaiting takeoff. He looked at his ticket, then at the gentleman sitting by the window, then back at his ticket, then back at the gentleman.

"I have 17-F," he stated, getting the other's attention. "I believe you're in my seat."

"No, I'm in 17-D. Says so right here." He took out his own ticket and showed it to the man in the aisle.

"Yes, but 17-D is the aisle seat. You see, the seating runs from side to side, A-B-C and then D-E-F. A and F are the window seats, and C and D are the aisle seats."

"Nonsense. I asked them for a window seat, so this must be it. Seat 17-D, Flight 501 to St. Louis."

"Oh. Then you're definitely out of place. All the seats going to St. Louis are in the middle row."

A teenager approached an airline ticket desk at the Indianapolis airport to inquire about an afternoon flight to Seattle. Without explaining to him the different time zones—Seattle is three hours behind—the agent punched a few keys on the computer and announced, "You can catch a flight at 5:02 P.M. nonstop to Seattle. It arrives at 5:24 P.M.."

The youth rubbed his chin. "The plane leaves here at 5:02 P.M. and gets to Seattle at 5:24 P.M.?"

"Yes."

"Today?"

"That's correct. Would you like to purchase a ticket?"

"No, I think I'll walk over here and watch that plane take off one time."

After watching a news account of an airline crash, a teenager was asking his mother about the vital "black box" that's so important to accident investigators.

"It contains a complete record of the plane's diagnostics right up to the instant of the crash," she explained.

"Why isn't it destroyed on impact?"

"Because it's encased in a very special alloy material, I'm sure."

"Then why can't they make the whole airplane out of that material?"

A nervous passenger decided to spring for one of those on-the-spot, low-investment-high-benefits insurance policies at the airport before her plane departed. Then she had time for a quick lunch, so she stopped at a Chinese diner along the terminal walk. Her eyes widened when she read the fortune cookie: "Today's investment will pay big dividends!"

For ten dollars, visitors to the country fair could ride in a barnstormer's biplane. An aging farm couple who'd never traveled outside the county thought they might like to take the opportunity to fly, just for posterity. But they were more than a little afraid.

"Tell you what," the barnstormer offered, perceiving their nervousness. "You can ride together, and I'll charge you only five dollars. Just promise me you won't scream or try to tell me how to fly my plane."

They accepted his offer and proceeded with the thrill of their lives. Through a wild series of loops and rolls, the pilot never heard a sound from his backseat companions.

"Wow, Pop, you were just great!" shouted the pilot over his shoulder as he landed the plane. "I thought for sure you'd both holler when we made that nosedive."

"That wasn't so bad," yelled the farmer. "But I almost did break my promise a few minutes before that, when my wife fell out of the airplane."

A rookie flight attendant was so nervous he was dropping trays, spilling drinks on passengers, and stumbling into his colleagues in the aisles.

"Calm down," said another attendant, drawing him aside in the galley. "You're behaving as if you've never flown before."

"I've flown lots of times," he responded. "But this afternoon before we took off, I got to examine all the restricted areas of the plane for the first time in my life. Just looking around gave me a terrible panic attack."

"Why? It's just another airliner."

"Don't you realize," he said, "that virtually every little part of this thing was supplied by the lowest bidder?"

AUTOMOBILES

A woman waited at a garage as mechanics scoured her car engine, trying in vain to pinpoint the problem. At length, a parrot in a corner cage sang out, "It's the thermostat."

"We've already checked the thermostat," grumbled one of the mechanics.

"It's the fan belt," the parrot ventured.

"No problem with the fan belt," said the other mechanic.

"It's the heat pump," said the parrot.

"It's not the heat pump!" shouted the first mechanic, exasperated.

The woman was astounded by this exchange. "I've never heard of a bird so intelligent," she said.

"He's completely worthless," countered the second mechanic. "He'll talk your ear off, but he doesn't know the first thing about car engines."

A rich suburbanite had car trouble while on a mountain holiday. He puttered into the yard of a rickety roadside filling station and called to the greasy, bearded attendant, "Have you had any experience with BMWs?"

"Buddy, if I could work on cars like that, I don't reckon I'd be here."

"The earth is round," the teacher said, "which means the surface of the earth is gradually curved."

"That explains it!" shouted Marcia.

"Explains what?"

"That explains why Mom's car pulls to the right."

BIRDS

Several buzzards had been circling all day, looking for a dead animal carcass to eat. As night approached, one wearily suggested to the others, "Let's just kill some small animal and eat it. If we don't, we'll all die of starvation."

"Buzzards can't do that," croaked a second.

"Says who?"

"I read it in the nature encyclopedia."

Two women sat on a park bench. One was immersed in the newspaper, the other admiring the beauty of the falling orange leaves, the cool September breeze, the squirrels chattering, and a million birds singing. "Oh, this is so wonderful," she couldn't help remarking. "Don't you just love the music of the birds?"

The other turned to her with a questioning frown. "Couldn't hear what you said. Can't hear anything at all, with these obnoxious birds and squirrels making such a racket."

A duck waddled into a country grocery store and asked the clerk, "Do you sell duck food?"

"Of course not," replied the clerk. "We sell groceries to humans, not ducks."

The next day the duck returned and asked again, "Do you sell duck food?"

Annoyed, the clerk snapped, "No! No duck food."

When the duck returned the next day and posed the same question, the clerk threatened, "I've told you this is a grocery store for people, not birds. If you ever come back in here and ask me that stupid question again, I'm going to nail one of your webbed feet to the floor and laugh while you walk around in circles."

The next day the duck was back. "Do you sell nails?"

The clerk, miffed, replied, "Of course not. This is a grocery store, not a hardware store."

Upon which the duck asked, "Do you sell duck food?"

CARPENTERS

Dad was pounding furiously
with a hammer on a back porch
wood project. Dogs barked. Neighbors phoned to complain.
Items hanging on the wall were rocked off their mounts.

His two children watched as the family's portable
weather station crashed to the floor. One child turned to the
other and asked, "Is this what weather broadcasters mean
when they say the barometer is falling?"

At a building site, a load of suspended lumber broke from
a hoist and fell to the ground, burying a carpenter. Before
his shocked coworkers could get to him, he rose from the
rubble, dusted his overalls, and hollered at the crane operator, "You idiot! You made me bite my lip!"

A policeman watched suspiciously as a man stepped out of
a van, holding his hands about two feet apart. The man
hurried down the street; the policeman followed. At the
entrance to a building supply store, the suspect—hands still
apart—waited until a customer came through the door. He
darted through the open door behind the other person,
seemingly afraid to touch the door with either hand.

The officer quietly entered the store behind him, just
in time to hear the stranger tell a clerk, "I need half a dozen
three-by-fours cut exactly this long."

CELEBRITIES & DIGNITARIES

Two rival candidates for a local government seat happened to meet at a taxi stand. Smith was a wealthy veteran of city hall politics, Brown a middle-income political novice.

"I hate to tell you this, Son," said Smith, condescending to offer a bit of frank advice, "but you need money if you ever want to run a successful campaign in this city. *Lots* of money. See this?" He took a wad of bills from a coat pocket. "I always carry plenty of cash and spread it around liberally. For example, when my cabby drops me off, I'll give him a wink, a smile, and a five-dollar-bill, and let him know I'm counting on his vote."

Young Brown got to thinking about the tactic and came up with a shoestring-budget variation. When his own cab driver dropped him off, he quickly stepped out the door without leaving any tip at all. "Be sure to vote for Smith in the city council race next Tuesday," he called over his shoulder.

One candidate at a political rally held the podium a full forty minutes with what had to be the most meaningless, boring speech in the county's history. Finally, he concluded and asked if anyone in the audience had a question.

"I do," piped up a voice. "Who's your opponent?"

The actor was talented, but unknown. A few minor roles in commercials and Grade B films were encouraging to his ego. But the fact was, he couldn't make his monthly rent payment.

"Don't you realize," he explained to his pragmatic landlord, "that within a year or two, my fans will be flocking to this address, just to view the apartment where such a great talent once lived?"

"I expect my rent in two days," said the landlord. "If I don't get paid, on the third day, your fans may proceed to come around and view the apartment where you once lived."

A candidate and his wife fell into the hotel bed at the end of a long day on the campaign trail.

"I'm exhausted," groaned the wife.

"I think I have more right to be exhausted than you do," complained the candidate. "I delivered six speeches in six no-count little towns today."

"And I had to listen to the same message six times."

The successful novelist, being interviewed on a TV talk show, lamented of burnout and self-doubt. "After twelve books and seven to eight million dollars in royalties, I finally realize I haven't the slightest talent for writing. Every one of my plots is just a rehash of things I've read by other writers."

"Are you telling us," hazarded the host, "that you're retiring?"

"Oh, of course not! Imagine what that would do to my reputation!"

CHILDREN

Father: "You never know what you can do until you try."
Son: "I guess you never know what you *can't* do until you try, either."

Mandy came crying to her dad. Between sobs, she explained that she'd traded her pet kitten Jingles to the children at the refreshment stand down the street for a cold drink.

"I see," he said, knowingly. "And now you miss little Jingles, don't you?"

"No," she said, "but I'm still thirsty, and I don't have anything else to trade."

Two mothers were comparing child-rearing notes. "I just can't seem to get my children's attention," said one. "They stay mesmerized in front of the TV set. I say things to them and call for them, and they're oblivious to every word."

"Try sitting in an easy chair and looking like you're relaxed," said the other. "That gets my children's attention without fail."

After being punished for losing his temper, a little boy ventured to ask his mother, "Please explain to me the difference between my foul temper and your worn nerves."

A father was scolding his children because they spent most of their summer days watching television. "Don't you know laziness is a trap? You'll never amount to anything if you fall into lazy habits. It's hard work that pays off."

The oldest child replied, "I know it'll pay off when we grow up. But for now, being lazy seems to pay off a lot better."

The tradition in the farm family was that when one of the boys misbehaved, he got a switching. And to drive the point home, he was required to go outside and cut his own switch.

Thus, bad little Ernie was sent out the door to select his means of punishment. Gone for several minutes, he finally returned with no switch—but with a handful of rocks.

"I couldn't find a good switch for you, Pa," he said. "Why don't you just stone me?"

A little boy took the chair at the barber shop.

"How would you like your hair cut today, Son?" asked the barber.

"Oh, do it like you do Daddy's, with the big hole at the back."

Micki's parents received a disturbing note from her second-grade teacher:

"Micki is an excellent student," the teacher began, "but when we have art and coloring projects, she draws everything in dark blue. Sky, grass, flowers, people, houses, kittens, cars, buildings, sun, moon, trees—it's all dark blue. This is unusual for a second-grader. Can you think of any explanation? If she's having some sort of emotional problem, we need to get to the bottom of it."

That night, the parents sat down with Micki and asked her why all her pictures were rendered in dark blue. Why was that such a special color to her? they asked.

"Well," she began, "I wasn't going to tell you. But see, about two weeks ago I lost my box of crayons. The only one left is the dark blue one I found in the front compartment of my backpack. . . ."

"I've never seen a hand so filthy," Mother said to Sammy when he came in from playing.

"Then take a look at this one," said Sammy, holding up his other hand.

An eighth grader was visibly frustrated as he struggled with his homework. Finally, he slammed the textbook shut, threw down his pencil, and announced to his parents, "I've decided I'm a conscientious objector."

"Why did you decide that?" his father asked.

"Because wars create too much history."

Six-year-old Alison was riding in the car with her mother. Mom bumped the signal light lever and prepared to make a turn. Alison was annoyed by the clicking cadence the signal device emitted from the dashboard.

"Mom, why in the world do you turn that thing on?"

"To let other drivers know I'm going to turn, Dear."

"But Mom, nobody can hear it but you and me."

The mother was furious. "Ricky," she called to her son, "last night when I turned out the kitchen light and went to bed, there were four Twinkie packages in the cookie jar.

This morning there are only two. What do you know about this?"

"Well, it was kinda dark," Ricky confessed. "I only saw two packages."

Two children were shouting at each other and were at the point of blows when Mom entered the playroom. "You two are always arguing," she scolded. "You need to learn to agree on things."

"We do agree," said one.

"Yeah," snarled the other. "We both agree we want the box of crayons *right now.*"

"Owwww!" screamed six-year-old Mindy.

"What is it?" her mother called from the kitchen.

"The baby pulled my hair."

Mother came in to comfort Mindy. "Don't be angry at the baby," she said. "He doesn't understand that it hurts when he pulls your hair."

She'd no sooner returned to the kitchen when there came another shriek, this time from the toddler. Returning to the playroom, she was confronted by Mindy, who explained, "Now he understands."

"But why can't I talk inside the library?" Mandy asked her mother.

"Because you have to be quiet. Noise is a distraction. The people around you can't read."

"Can't read? Then why are they at the library?"

A child was thoroughly bored after being stuck inside the house all day because of rain. "Mom," she whined, "why does God send the rain anyway?"

"To nourish the earth," her mother said. "That's how the crops and the flowers and the trees grow."

"But why does He make it rain in the parking lot where I like to go skating?"

A mother was trying to impress upon her children the need for safety while playing. "You remember our neighbor Barry," she said somberly. "He was riding his roller skates and wasn't paying attention where he was going. He hit a tree and ended up in the hospital, and now his right leg's paralyzed. He'll never skate again."

Little Jeannie was suddenly quite interested. "So what became of his skates?"

A mother came home from shopping and found her newly baked pie dug out crudely from the center. The crime tool—a gooey spoon—lay in the sink. Crumbs were all over the kitchen counter and floor.

She called her son into the kitchen. "Peter," she said sternly, "you promised me you wouldn't touch that pie before dinner."

Peter hung his head.

"And I promised you I'd spank you if you did," she continued.

Peter brightened. "Now that I've broken my promise," he offered, "I think it'll be all right for you to break yours, too!"

CHURCH HUMOR

"Lord," came the prayer, "so far today, so good. I haven't sworn, stolen anything, boasted, gotten angry at anyone, or even had any evil thoughts.

"But now comes the test, and I implore your help. I have to get up and go to work. . . ."

Two children were among worshipers filing into the sanctuary the first Sunday morning in January. One frowned and pointed to the Christmas tree, which still stood in honor of the Advent season. "Why is the Christmas tree still up?"

"Because it isn't December 25 yet," the other child answered.

"Does anyone know the meaning of the word 'epistle'?" the Sunday school teacher asked.

"I believe those were the wives of the apostles," guessed one student.

A family who'd just moved into town spent Sunday mornings for the first few months visiting different churches.

Returning home after one service, the eight year old remarked, "We definitely don't wanna join that church."

"Why not?" asked Dad.

"This is the third time we've been there, and it's rained every time."

A country church held a covered dish supper on opening night of its revival series. The guest preacher was invited to lead the food line, but he declined. "I can't eat a big meal before I preach," he explained to the congregation. "It detracts from my ability to deliver a good sermon."

Two hours later, several women were cleaning up the church kitchen. "I declare," mumbled one, "I believe that preacher might as well have ate his fill at suppertime."

"King David used to be a hero of mine, but not anymore," little Brodie told his mother after church one Sunday.

"Why not, Son?"

"I learned today that he killed the Jolly Green Giant."

Torrential rains were swiftly flooding the town's streets. A preacher sat on his porch watching the deluge. As the rising water approached his front steps, a rescue squad boat motored by. "Come aboard, Preacher!" shouted one of the officials. "We'll carry you to safety."

"I'm safe enough," the preacher replied. "I'm trusting the Lord to protect me and my home."

Half an hour later the water was up to the porch floor. Another boat glided past. "Jump aboard, Preacher! It's going to get worse!"

"I'm not afraid, friends. The Lord will deliver me from drowning."

Late in the day the flood had almost engulfed the town's buildings. The preacher was on the roof, clinging to the chimney, when a helicopter hovered overhead. A rope was cranked down to the pitiful victim—and astonishingly, the preacher waved the crew away. "The Lord Himself will save me," he declared.

As darkness descended, the preacher was swept to his death.

The next thing he knew, he was at heaven's gate, waiting at the desk of St. Peter. The venerable saint looked up from his writing. "You!" he exclaimed. "What are you doing here already?"

"Well," the preacher stammered, "I was down there in the flood, waiting for the Lord to rescue me, and finally the water just got too high and. . ."

"Saints, man! We sent you two boats and a helicopter!"

"Can anyone name the Roman emperor who was most notorious for persecuting early Christians?" the Sunday school teacher asked.

"Nero," promptly responded one youth.

"That's right. What were some of the things he did?"

"He tortured the prisoners in Rome."

"And do you know how he tortured them?"

"He played the fiddle at 'em."

Little Rodney seemed troubled at Sunday dinner. "What is it, Son?" his dad asked.

"I really didn't like that violent hymn we sang in church," Rodney said.

"Violent? What hymn was violent?"

"You know. The one that goes, 'There is a bomb in Gilead.' "

Sunday school teacher: "What became of Tyre?"
Pupil: "The Lord punctured it."

"Mom, are there animals in heaven?"

"What kinds of animals?"

"Regular animals, like cows and bees."

"I'm not sure about that. I doubt they'll be *necessary* in heaven."

"Then where are we going to get enough milk and honey for everybody?"

The Sunday school teacher had her children draw a picture of the manger scene for Christmas week. The students all drew wonderful variations on the same basic theme: Mary and Joseph, the infant in the cradle, the animals, the shepherds, the wise men. Something about little Wayne's drawing baffled her, though.

"What's that large box in front of everyone, with the lines coming out of the top?" she asked.

"That's their television set," Wayne said proudly.

A new employee was being shown the ropes at the office.

"What our management looks for more than anything else," said the supervisor, "is for everyone here to be methodical. You can get by with a few deficiencies in other regards, but you absolutely *must* be methodical."

The newcomer, stunned, said, "Well, I may as well turn in my resignation right now."

"But you haven't even started work!"

"No, and I don't plan to. I've been a deep-water Baptist all my life, and I don't see any good reason to become a Methodical at this point in time."

Casey approached her Sunday school teacher after class with a question: "If the people of Israel were Israelites and the people of Canaan were Canaanites, are parasites what we call the people living in Paris?"

A child was watching his mother sift through and delete a long list of junk E-mail on the computer screen.

"This reminds me of the Lord's Prayer," the child said.

"What do you mean?"

"You know. That part about 'deliver us from E-mail.'"

COLLEGE

Father: "You're telling me your entire class got an A in philosophy? How?"

Daughter: "We proved the professor didn't exist. What could she do?"

The parents of a first-year college student received this note from their child:

> Dear Mom & Dad,
>   Univer$ity life i$ $o wonderful! Cla$$e$ are intere$ting. Cla$$mate$ are the be$t. The only thing I need right now i$ a little ca$h.
>   Love,
>   Dabney

After deliberating, they drafted an appropriate response:

> Dear Dabney,
>   NOt much is happening here on the NOrth side of town since you left for NOrth-western U. See you at Thanksgiving in NOvember? Loved your letter. Write aNOther one when you have time. Have to go NOw.
>   Love,
>   Mom & Dad

COMPUTERS

Two information services managers were complaining about their work.

"If our computers could think for themselves, my problems would be over," said one.

"If my technical staff could think for themselves, so would mine," said the other.

While trying to run four different programs in memory and juggle data between them, a typist saw this error message appear on-screen: FORGET IT. YOU'RE ASKING TOO MUCH.

Another computer operator received this error message: THREE THINGS IN LIFE ARE GUARANTEED: TAXES, DEATH, AND COMPUTER CRASHES. GUESS WHICH ONE JUST HAPPENED.

"I'll just never be able to use computers," whined Grant. "I don't think I have the basic aptitude for them."

"But they're so easy to use these days," said Cameron. "A lot of times, the only thing you have to do to answer the computer's prompts is 'PRESS ANY KEY.' "

"Yeah, that's one of my problems. I've never been able to find the 'ANY' key."

What's the first symptom of a computer getting old?
Memory problems.

A sales clerk in an electronics store noticed a customer staring at a display unit. The display was a voice-activated computer with a built-in microphone.

The clerk moseyed over and whispered to the baffled customer, "It's a voice computer. You simply speak to it, as you would to a person. The first thing it needs to know, in order to begin operating, is your name."

The customer watched the clerk walk away, then leaned near the computer and whispered, "My name's Sam Smith. What's your name?"

CRIME

Judge, to repeat offender:
  "What are you charged with
  this time, Mr. Smith?"
Smith: "I was just trying to get my Christmas shopping
  done early."
Police officer: "Yes—before the store opened, Your
  Honor."

Several security guards were scratching their heads in the
aftermath of a bank robbery.

"But how could they have gotten away?" one wondered aloud. "We had all the exits guarded."

"I think they must have gone out the entrance," suggested another.

A poor bookseller walked through Central Park on his way
home each evening. One Monday a masked man jumped
from behind a tree. "Give me your money!"

"I have no money. I'm just a poor bookseller. Here's
my wallet; see for yourself."

Finding the wallet and the victim's pockets all empty,
the bandit grumbled and ran off into the darkening
shrubbery.

The next Monday the same bandit accosted the

bookseller. "Give me your money!" Again he made off without a dime.

This happened each Monday evening for a month. Finally the bookseller said to him, "Look, you recognize me. You know I'm only a poor bookseller, and I don't carry any money at all. Why do you waste your time and risk getting caught every Monday?"

The robber replied, "I'm still practicing, and you don't seem to mind too much."

After weeks of agonizing physical training, police academy cadets still hadn't been admitted to the firing range.

"I don't get it," huffed one trainee to another as they pounded out yet another five-mile jog.

"What do you mean?"

"We still don't know how to protect people and property, but we're getting real good at running away."

"The prosecutor says she can produce five witnesses who saw you running from the bank with the money bags," a defense lawyer confided to a suspect.

"That's nothing," said the suspect. "I can produce five hundred witnesses who didn't see me running from the bank."

DEFINITIONS

abash: a high school graduation party.

account: a countess's husband.

alarm clock: a machine invented to scare the daylights into you.

alimony: the place where Crockett, Bowie, Travis, and about 180 other guys died fighting for Texas's independence.

antique: an item your grandparents bought, your parents got rid of, and you're buying again.

argument: a fight over who can get in the last word first.

bargain: something that's so cheap you can't resist it, even though you can't use it and don't really want it.

barium: what we do to most people when they die.

beta tester: anyone who uses any computer program.

blackout: an abnormality of electrical power that turns a two-thousand-dollar computer system into so many paperweights.

business meeting: a time for people to talk about what they're supposed to be doing.

catalogs: rails used to construct cow fences.

confidence: the human quality that comes before experience.

courtesy: the art of yawning with your mouth closed.

derange: land where de buffalo roam.

discretion: the art of being wiser than anyone while letting no one know it.

encores: songs performers have to sing until they finally get one right.

etc.: an abbreviation used to make people think you have additional information.

experience: something you've acquired after it's too late to do you much good.

expert: someone who knows the answers—assuming you ask the right questions.

expiration: the process of not breathing.

furlough: snore duty.

goblet: a young turkey.

gossipers: people who believe anything they overhear.

graduate school: the approximate point at which a university student ceases dependency on parents and commences dependency on spouse.

headache: a pain reliever deficiency.

hospital: the place to wind up people who are run-down.

import: an inland seaport.

impossibility: something no one can do until someone does it.

income tax: the cause of spring fever.

know-it-all: a person who knows everything there is to know about nothing.

love: what happens when imagination overpowers common sense.

low mileage: what you get when your car won't start.

middle age: when you're sitting home alone on Friday night and you hope the phone doesn't ring.

miser: a person who lives poor and dies rich.

misnomer: the correct word for an incorrect word.

money: a device by which parents stay in touch with their college children.

mundane: the day after a wonderful weekend.

nail: what amateur carpenters replace with their thumb while the hammer is in motion.

nervous disorder: a hereditary condition parents inherit from their teenage children.

newscast: one place where good rarely triumphs over evil.

nothing: the presence of absence.

nuclear scientist: a professional with a lot of ions in the fire.

opportunist: a mail carrier who enjoys the view when treed by a dog.

opportunity: something that knocks but doesn't turn the door handle.

optimist: someone blithely ignorant of how serious a crisis really is.

orthodontist: a doctor who braces children and straps parents.

oxygen: a little-used form of the word "ox."

pessimist: a former optimist.

Phoenicia: an ancient Mediterranean seaport remembered for its dearth of telephone communication.

phonetic: an example of a word that isn't spelled the way it sounds.

practical nurse: a nurse who marries a wealthy patient.

quality control: corporate term for "nagging."

quicksilver: what the Lone Ranger says when he needs to go fast.

Rome: what buffalo do.

scorekeeper: the symphony orchestra's librarian.

Shanghai: opposite of Shanglow.

spice: plural of spouse.

steering committee: a panel of individuals who aren't capable of driving by themselves.

subordinate clause: the grammatically correct term for Santa Claus's assistant.

tact: the knack for knowing exactly what not to say.

teamwork: getting a group of individuals to do what one person tells them to.

time: the component of life that keeps everything bad from happening to you all at once.

tragic opera: a musical-theatrical performance in which most of the characters sing and then die.

unbreakable: an adjective used to describe many toys—with the implied disclaimer that any warranties are voided where children are present.

upward adjustment: a price increase.

vegetarian: a person who refuses to eat meat in public.

Venice: one of the planets.

wake-up call: the issue of mind over mattress.

wastebasket: a receptacle near which trash is tossed.

wide receiver: a twelve-foot TV antenna.

yacht: a floating credit liability.

DIETING

Jeff: "Why are you so eager to meet the right woman, settle down, and get married?"
Mike: "So I can stop dieting."

"Wilma will never make much progress with her diet."

"Why do you think not?"

"She has some bizarre ideas about calorie counting. For example, she thinks if you have a slice of chocolate cake with a cup of low-calorie instant cocoa, they cancel out each other."

A couple was enjoying a dinner party at the home of friends. Near the end of the meal, the wife slapped her husband's arm.

"That's the third time you've gone for dessert," she said. "The hostess must think you're an absolute pig."

"I doubt that," the husband said. "I've been telling her it's for you."

"I thought you said you were counting calories," remarked Mrs. Bowker, scowling as her friend Mrs. Halburton enjoyed her second chocolate shake at the ice cream shop.

"I am indeed," said Mrs. Halburton between slurps. "So far today, this makes 7,750."

DOCTORS & PATIENTS

Doctor: "That's a horrible gash on your skull. What happened?"
Child: "My sister hit me with some tomatoes."
Doctor: "That's incredible. I've never seen a tomato cut before."
Child: "Well, these were in a can."

A young man brought his wife to a small town doctor's office in an emergency. The nurses escorted the woman to the examination area, and the husband anxiously took a seat in the lobby.

For the next few minutes, he could hear the doctor bark an unsettling string of orders to the staff. First it was "Screwdriver!" Then "Knife!" Then "Pliers!"

When he heard "Sledge hammer!" the young man could bear the tension no longer. He burst into the examination room and shrieked, "Doctor, what's *wrong* with her?"

"We have no idea," the doctor said. "Right now, we're still trying to open the medicine cabinet."

Doctor: "So you haven't been able to sleep well?"
Patient: "I sleep fine during the night, but during my afternoon naps, I just can't keep my eyes closed."

"Doc, it's my husband!" shrieked a woman into the phone. "I served lasagna for dinner last night, and this morning he's turned all blue!"

"Sing him a song," suggested the doctor. "Tell him a joke."

Doctor: "What seems to be the problem with little Micah today?"
Panicked Parent: "We think he swallowed a bullet!"
Doctor: "For heaven's sake, stop pointing him at me!"

A pharmacist was squinting and holding the prescription slip up to the light. Finally she took up a magnifier in a futile effort to read it.

"We don't think too highly of this particular doctor," she told the customer, "but there's one thing he obviously can do better than anyone else on the planet."

"What's that?"

"Read his own handwriting."

A doctor's receptionist answered the phone and was screamed at by an excited man at the other end of the line.

"My wife's in labor!" he yelled. "I think she's going to deliver any minute now."

"Please calm down," the receptionist said. "Try to relax and give me some basic information. Is this her first child?"

"No, no! I'm her husband!"

An auto mechanic in the hospital was chatting nervously with his surgeon while being prepped for an operation. "Sometimes I wish I'd gone into your line of work," he told the doctor. "Everything you doctors do is so cut and dried and tidy. With me, I spend half a day taking an engine apart and putting it back together, and it seems I always have a couple of parts left over."

"Yes," said the surgeon. "I know the feeling."

Doctors in the emergency room examined the incoming patient, a hit-and-run victim, with concern. Several broken ribs, a fractured femur, and various other internal and external injuries indicated tedious surgical procedures were in order. It was amazing the patient was momentarily conscious.

"Are you allergic to anything?" one doctor asked.

"Yes," she replied weakly.

"What's that?"

"Oncoming trucks."

DRIVERS

A driving student was poring over the handbook just before taking the written exam. Suddenly he got up and hurried from the training room.

"Hey, where are you going?" the instructor demanded.

"I'm outta here, man. Gotta phone my parents, like, right now!"

"What's the matter? Don't you want to earn your driver's license?"

"Doesn't matter. First thing we have to do is move, and I mean *today!*"

"Move? You mean move your family?"

"Yep. Lock, stock, and motorcycle. Find a new house."

"What on earth for?"

"It says in that book that 90 percent of all traffic fatalities in the United States occur within five miles of home."

A stranger drove to a halt beside a pedestrian in a tiny, remote village. Lost and in a hurry, the driver had no desire to engage in conversation with the locals; he only wanted quick directions.

"Hey, idiot," he snapped. "Can you tell me how to get to Portland?"

"Yes," the villager said, before turning to cross the street and disappear inside a shop door.

"My Dad must be a pretty bad driver," said Brad.

"What do you mean?" asked Bret.

"I was with him when he got pulled over for speeding yesterday. The officer recognized him and wrote him out a season ticket."

Some teenage friends were marveling at the scene of an accident where one of them miraculously had walked away from the mishap without a scratch the night before.

"Wow, that was some smashup," said one.

"Totaled the car," said another.

"How'd it happen?" asked a third.

The victim pointed to a tilted telephone pole. "See that?"

"Yeah."

"I didn't."

A patrol officer chased down a speeder after a thirty-mile adventure on the interstate—only after the speeder had run out of gas.

"Congratulations," said the officer sarcastically. "You hit 163 miles per hour. I didn't think a little subcompact like that could give me such a run."

"And congratulations to you. I didn't think you could keep up."

A team of paramedics loaded a dazed auto accident victim into the ambulance.

"I don't understand it," the stunned patient moaned. "I'm sure I had the right-of-way."

"Yes," said a medic, "but the other driver had the eighteen-wheeler."

ECONOMICS

When you need to borrow money, borrow it from a pessimist. Pessimists don't expect it to be returned.

A woman was extremely impressed with a gold watch in a jewelry shop. "You say this is only $29.95," she remarked to the jeweler. "There must be something wrong with it."

"No, Madam. It's simply marked down to a dollar above cost."

"You're telling me you paid only $29 for it yourself?"

"That's correct, Madam."

"Nonsense. If that's true, how could you possibly make a living?"

"You forget, Madam, this is also a repair shop."

Money talks, but it has a one-word vocabulary: *good-bye.*

After successfully getting their big line items approved in the congressional spending package, two lobbyists were celebrating at a Washington restaurant.

"You know," mused one, "it's a crying shame our grand-children and great-grandchildren haven't been born yet so they can see the terrific things the government's doing with their money."

FAMILY TIES

She: "Our problem is that we're just not communicating."
He: "I don't wanna discuss it."

A farmer's wife went into a coma at home, and he summoned the doctor.

"She's gone," said the doc after examining the woman. "I'm very sorry. I'll call the funeral home for you."

The morticians carried the body down the porch steps and started to round the corner of the house into the driveway when the lead bearer suddenly lurched to avoid a holly bush, lost his balance, and dropped his end of the stretcher. The jolt brought the woman back to consciousness. In a week, she'd made a full recovery and was back at the farm.

Several years later she again went into a coma. This time, the doctor sadly assured her husband, she was unquestionably dead.

The undertakers were summoned. As the stretcher bearers inched down the steps and headed for the driveway with the corpse, the farmer cautioned, "Watch out for that holly bush."

Mother was amused when she heard her six-year-old son whining to a friend: "I don't get it. My sister insists she has

45

three brothers. But I'm in the same family, and I count only two brothers. . . ."

A man died and, as he'd requested, was cremated. But he didn't specify what was to be done with the ashes. They ended up in an hour glass in his widow's kitchen cabinet.

"Why do you keep him there?" a friend asked.

"Well, he never was good for much when he was alive. At least now I can put him to work timing the casseroles."

When he went to visit his cousin in the big city, Farmer Dan was amazed at the dozens of cats loitering around the apartment complex. "Why don't you shoo 'em?" he asked his cousin.

"Here in town, we let the cats go barefoot."

Grandson: "Grandma, how many brothers and sisters did you have?"

Grandma: "Eleven brothers and eight sisters."

Grandson: "Wow! I bet yours was the biggest family in the whole town."

Grandma: "Yes. I expect that's why they built the new school next to our house."

At three in the morning, a young wife shook her husband awake.

"What is it?" he asked groggily.

"The baby," she reminded him.

The husband sat up and listened a full minute. "But I don't hear her crying," he protested.

"I know. It's your turn to go see why not."

Two cousins were having a friendly chat when one blurted, out of the blue, "Man, I need to borrow one hundred dollars from somebody by the end of the week."

"Really?"

"I sure do. Don't know who to turn to, either."

"I'm very glad to hear that. It sounded for a moment like you were gonna turn to me."

Smith: "I understand the Family Court social worker was at your house asking questions the other day."

Jones: "Yeah, my son was telling everyone at school he came from a broken home."

Smith: "Broken home? I thought you and Angie were happily married."

Jones: "We are. But the cement's coming loose between the blocks in our basement."

"Now, Charles, come give your old aunt a kiss before she goes," Aunt Meg said, putting on her gloves.

Charles shook his head.

"Come, now, Charles." She took a quarter from her purse and smiled. "I'll give you this if you'll just give me one little kiss on the cheek, like a good boy."

"Nah," Charles said. "Mom gives me that much just for eating Brussels sprouts."

Mr. Brown was seen each weekday morning peddling a bicycle to the shuttle stop, briefcase under his arm. His wife ran after him, perspiring heavily and gasping for breath.

One day a neighbor confronted Brown with his thoughtless behavior. "Why is it you ride the bicycle and she has to run?"

"She doesn't own a bike," was the offhanded reply.

FARM & GARDEN

A school class was on a field trip to the farm.

"Look, look!" cried a student, pointing. "There's a little cow with no horns! All the other cows have horns. Why doesn't this one?"

The farmer puffed his pipe and drawled an explanation. "There are a lot of reasons some cows don't have horns," he said. "It might depend on the breed; some cattle breeds are horned and some aren't. Or it could be the cow's age; some don't grow horns until they're adults. And in some cases, cows that once had horns have lost them in collisions, or their owners have removed them for one reason or another.

"But in the case of this young cow here, it doesn't have horns because it's a colt."

"I want to start a garden, but my yard's a little problematic," a customer told the proprietor at the yard and garden center. "I get blazing afternoon sunshine for about two hours, but otherwise it's all shade."

"What kind of soil?" asked the proprietor.

"Hard clay, lot of rocks. What do you recommend I plant?"

"Hmmm," mused the store's owner. "Why don't you look down aisle B? We've got a big new supply of birdbaths and flagpoles. . . ."

A farmer chided his teenage grandson, "Your generation has gotten lazy. When I was fifteen, I thought nothing of getting up at daybreak to milk the cows."

"I don't think much of it, either," said the youth.

A stranger frantically ran up to a farmer's door, pounded his fist and demanded, "Where's the nearest railroad station, and what time's the next train to the city?"

The farmer thought a moment. "Cut through my back hayfield, and you ought to reach the crossroads station in time for the 5:40. Actually, if my bull spots you, I expect you'll make the 5:15."

Farmer Brown: "Did you lose much in that last tornado?"
Farmer Jones: "Lost the henhouse and all the chickens.
But that was all right—I ended up with three new cows and somebody's pickup truck."

Farmer Tanner rang up a neighbor on the telephone. "My best milking cow has a fever," he said. "How did you treat your ol' Bessie when she got sick last winter?"

"Well, I made up a mixture of half cod liver oil and half turpentine and put it in with her food once a day for four days."

"Thanks. I'll try it."

Farmer Tanner hung up the phone and proceeded to treat his cow. Shockingly, after four days of the medicine compound, the cow died.

He rang up his neighbor again. "Hey, I did exactly what you said with the cod liver oil and turpentine mixture, but my cow just died."

"Yep. So did ol' Bessie."

GROWNUPS

"Mom, Dad just hit his thumb with a hammer."

"Oh, dear. What did he say?"

"You wouldn't want me to repeat any bad words, would you, Mom?"

"Certainly not."

"Well, then, he didn't say anything."

"Dad, there's something I've gotta tell you," Shane said, following his father inside the bait shop.

"Not now, Son. I have to select our fish bait."

Later, entering the convenience store, Shane tried again. "Hey, Dad—."

"Hold on, Son. I have to grab some lunch for our fishing trip."

At the gas station, Dad was filling the boat tank when Shane began, "Dad, there's something you really need to know. . . ."

"Just wait, Son. I need to pay for this gas so we can hit the road."

An hour later, as they sat in the boat catching fish, the father remembered his son's nagging. "What was it you were trying to tell me awhile ago?" he asked.

"Oh, not much. Just that your fly is open."

A five year old came into the kitchen and asked, "Mommy, can I have a slice of strawberry pie?"

"Now, Randall," his mother corrected, "you don't say 'can I have.' You say 'may I have.'"

"Okay. May I have a slice of strawberry pie?"

"And what do you say at the end?"

"Oh—may I have a slice of strawberry pie, please?"

"No, Dear. We'll be having dinner in less than an hour."

"Dad, which do you think is America's worst problem: ignorance or apathy?"

"Don't know. Don't really care, either."

HISTORY

"Who invented the bow and arrow?" asked the teacher.

"Cavemen!" cried Gary enthusiastically.

"Cavemen? And what do you suppose prompted cavemen to come up with the bow and arrow?"

"Er. . .somebody kept stealing the wheel?"

"What would be your definition of 'liberty'?" asked the civics teacher.

"That was the first choice of Patrick Henry."

History Teacher: "Who was the most famous Egyptian in history?"

Student: "The Mummy."

"What do you think was the most important invention in all of history?" the teacher asked his class.

"The automobile," said one student.

"The airplane," said another.

"The nuclear submarine," said the third.

"The credit card," said the fourth.

HUMAN NATURE

Harold: "My mom said it's only
 a coincidence that you and
 I have the same last name, because we're not related.
 Do you know what the word 'coincidence' means?"
George: "Nah, I was about to ask you what it means."

"You just don't know who to trust these days," said Mick.
"I put a dollar in a vending machine, and it gave me back
a Canadian quarter for change."

"That's too bad," said Nick. "A lot of businesses won't
accept those."

"I know. I got rid of it, though."

"How?"

"Left it as a tip at the coffee shop."

Three mice lugged their prize of cheese out to the shade
tree to enjoy a picnic lunch. Suddenly a dark cloud came
up, and it began raining heavily.

"We need an umbrella," said one. "Who's going back
to the house to get it?"

Each mouse was afraid that if he left the picnic, the
other two would eat all the cheese. Finally they resolved
the question by drawing straws. The loser hesitantly dis-
appeared into the driving rain.

The two other mice eyed the cheese hungrily. But being honest critters, they refrained from indulging before their friend returned with the umbrella.

The third mouse was gone for ten minutes. Then thirty minutes. Then an hour.

"Something's happened," said one of the waiting mice. "I don't think our friend's coming back today. We may as well dig into the cheese."

"I agree," said the other.

Just then the third mouse squeaked from behind the tree, "Touch that cheese, and I won't go for the umbrella!"

Mother: "Jack, you're always procrastinating. You *must* change."
Jack: "Sure, Mom. I'll change, I promise. I'll start Monday."

HUNTING

A man attired in camouflage entered a butcher shop.

"Can you sell me a couple of undressed ducks?" he asked.

"Well, no. We have no fresh ducks at the moment. I can sell you a nice selection of poultry broilers, though."

"Chickens!" the customer scoffed. "No way. I can't go home and tell my wife I bagged a couple of chickens!"

Paul: "Willie finally shot his first wild duck this morning."
Brad: "Reckon it won't be worth cookin'."
Paul: "Why not?"
Brad: "Must've been a very old duck, if it was flyin' low enough for Willie to shoot it."

Two easterners were hunting in the Rocky Mountain wilderness when a huge grizzly bear sprang onto their path, reared up, and roared.

One hunter was paralyzed with fright. The other kept his presence of mind and advised calmly, "Don't move a muscle. Just stand like a statue, and the bear will get bored and go away."

"H–h–how do you know?"

"Read it in a book about Lewis and Clark's expedition."

So they stood motionless. The bear didn't go away but

instead drew closer and roared more furiously.

"I–I–I think the bear must've read that same book!" stammered the frightened hunter.

Four hunters were bragging about the merits of their favorite blue tick hounds.

"My ol' Benny goes to the store for me," said one. "Always brings me back my favorite brand of tobacco."

"My dog Suzie buys our grits at that same store," said another. "I give her a five-dollar bill, and she brings me back the change first, then returns for the bag of grits."

"I send ol' Mack there for my shotgun shells," said the third. "He knows exactly what gauge and brand I want."

The fourth hunter said nothing until he was prompted by the others to try to top their tales.

"I reckon my dog ain't much to speak of, by comparison," he allowed. "He just sits in the store all day and operates the cash register."

LAWYERS & CLIENTS

A couple gaped at the TV as they watched their lawyer being interviewed during a newscast. The reporter wanted the attorney's comments for a local angle in a late-breaking Supreme Court decision.

"I wonder how in the world she got hold of our lawyer," the husband said, shaking his head. "I've been trying to get him to update our will for the last three weeks, and his secretary invariably says he's with clients."

"I love my profession," said the lawyer. "With each new client, it's a challenge, with a brand-new set of facts and a different solution. I never know what to do until I've studied the situation and researched the case law."

"Whereas in my profession," remarked the mortician sadly, "I know exactly what I'm going to do for all my clients before they even come through the door."

Two young attorneys fresh out of law school were sharing lunch. "I just got my first case!" one beamed excitedly.
"Oh? Who's the client?"
"Me!"

"You?!? You're representing yourself in your first case?"

"Yeah. I'm being sued."

"By whom?"

"By my dad."

"Your own *father* is suing you? What for?"

"For the fifty-five thousand dollars he spent sending me to law school."

A lawyer was cross-examining an elderly witness in a robbery case. He thought he'd capitalize on the probability that her eyesight left something to be desired.

"Mrs. Wilson, would you please tell us your age?"

"I'm seventy-eight years old," she said proudly.

"And have you ever worn eyeglasses?"

"I carry a pair in my purse, but I hardly ever need them."

"Is that so? Now, Mrs. Wilson, how far away from the scene of the crime were you standing?"

"I was down the street a little ways. They tell me it was sixty or seventy yards."

"Are you absolutely certain you can see things clearly at that distance?"

"I suppose so. We're 240,000 miles from the moon, and I can see that just fine on clear nights."

LOGIC

Two commercial bankers were having lunch. One was a twenty-year veteran of the finance industry, the other a novice just out of business school. The younger was picking the other's brain for advice.

"Mr. Morton, what usually happens when a person with a lot of money but no experience goes into partnership with a person who has no money but lots of experience?"

"Either the venture will fail altogether," advised the senior, "or the partner with the experience will end up with all the money."

Two friends were discussing a mutual acquaintance.

"I don't think she's really antisocial," said one.

"Nah," said the other. "She just despises humans."

MacDonald, an old highlander, was nonplused at his first encounter with a thermos bottle. "If ye put hot coffee in it, it keeps the coffee pipin' hot," delightedly explained his seven-year-old granddaughter. "If ye put in ice water, it keeps the water ice cold."

MacDonald shook his head. "Aye, I believe ye," he said. "But how does it know whether ye want it hot or cold. . . ?"

"How many officers do you have on your force?" a visiting relative asked a small-town police chief.

"Counting myself, there are three of us."

"Man, don't tell me this little nowhere of a crossroads needs three police officers!"

"If it weren't for us," responded the chief dryly, "it certainly would."

A retired volunteer was presented with an annual award at a community service banquet.

"I really don't deserve this," the honoree told the audience, "but then again, I expect I really don't deserve arthritis, either."

A very businesslike paperboy knocked on the door of a house. When a woman answered, he demanded, "You haven't paid for your paper all month. Pay up right now or you're off the route, and you'll be hearing from our collection agency."

The woman looked around her yard and answered, "I've paid you every week, in much the same way you deliver my newspaper. Look. There's a payment envelope in the bushes to the left, one in the bushes to the right, one up in the gutter of the porch, and one in the hole in my living room window."

Two archaeologists were pondering the inscription at the foot of the mummy's case. It read simply: 3 B.C.

"What can that possibly mean?" wondered the first archaeologist.

"Hmm. Could be the license tag of the guy who ran him down."

Reluctant bather: "You're sure there are no sharks along this beach?"

Lifeguard: "Highly unlikely. They don't get along with the alligators."

"Did I ever tell you about my adventures eradicating alligators from the streets of Manhattan?"

"There are no alligators on the streets of Manhattan."

"Nope. Not anymore."

A woman wrote a check at a department store.

"I'll have to ask you to identify yourself," the clerk said.

The customer took a small mirror from her handbag, looked into it keenly and pronounced, "Yes. That's definitely me."

Trisha: "Do you believe in smoking?"

Michele: "Well, I've seen it with my own eyes, several times."

Pessimist: "I'm a miserable failure. Always have been, always will be."

Optimist: "Maybe you just started at the bottom and felt comfortable there."

Two friends were discussing the relative merits of car models.

"I'm waiting for a car that'll last me a lifetime," said one.

"I hope to live longer than that," said the other.

"I don't think my right signal light is working," said Pam, stopping her car at a traffic light one evening. Asking brother Sam to check it, she flipped the blinker switch. Sam stuck his head out the passenger's window and reported, "It's working. . . . Wait a minute. . . . It's working. . . . Wait a minute. . . . It's working. . . ."

MEDIA

A newspaper ran a blistering editorial in which it stated, "We believe half the members of city council are swindlers."

City hall and its political supporters flooded the editor's phone line for three days. Finally, a retraction was promised. It read: "We now believe half the members of city council are not swindlers."

Teacher: "Why is television called a 'medium'?"
Student: "Because it's neither rare nor well-done."

Folks throughout the city knew they were in trouble when the new owners of the *Tribune* suavely altered the paper's time-honored motto to read: "All the News That's Fit for Us."

"How is Grace enjoying her retirement?"

"Well, she went back to work after a week."

"Oh, no! Why, she's been looking forward to retirement for years."

"That was before she saw what's on daytime television now."

What were the first words spoken after TV was invented?
"This is gonna be just another fad. . . ."

A cub reporter was dispatched to cover an earthquake scene. The devastation was extensive and horrible, with buildings crumbled, folks in shock, sporadic fires, and emergency workers racing hither and yon. Overwhelmed, the reporter waxed theological as she called in her story.

"Even God weeps tonight," she began dictating to her editor, "as He looks down at—"

"Forget the quake!" interrupted the editor. "Interview God. Is our photographer still around?"

Warren: "Today's news makes me sick."
Matt: "What paper do you read?"
Warren: *"USA Today."*
Matt: "Try *USA Yesterday.*"

MUSIC

"Cheryl is a true lover of classical music."

"I've figured that out. The 'William Tell Overture' is her favorite piece of music—and she doesn't know who the Lone Ranger is."

Two symphony critics were comparing notes after a concert. "The conductor was fantastic, I thought," said one. "Did you observe how the very first crescendo literally filled the music hall?"

"Yes," said the other. "A substantial number of the audience removed themselves to give it room."

What's the difference between bagpipes and a lawn mower?
You can tune a lawn mower.

A lady aboard a cruise ship was not impressed by the jazz trio in one of the shipboard restaurants. When her waiter came around, she asked, "Will they play anything I ask?"

"Of course, Madam."

"Then tell them to go play shuffleboard."

McLaramie: "Had a racket at home t'other evenin'.
    Family above us were stompin' the floor and just
    ahollerin' til the wee hours o' the marnin'."
McClintock: "Kept ye awake, did it?"
McLaramie: "No, fortunately, I was up already, playin'
    muh bagpipes."

A great pianist once was asked by an erstwhile child prodigy for his advice on how to become the greatest pianist in history.

"My best advice," said the older man, "is to begin practicing while you are very young, learn all you can from your elders and hopefully, by the time you've reached the end of your life, you will have attained your goal."

"But you were great before the age of twenty," the youngster protested.

"Perhaps," acknowledged his mentor. "But I never had to ask anyone's advice."

A couple was standing in the ticket line at the concert hall when the husband remarked, "I wish we'd brought along our piano bench."

"What in the world for?"

"Because the tickets are inside the seat."

The symphony musicians had little confidence in the person brought in to be their new conductor. Their fears were realized at the very first rehearsal. The conductor's wand was unsteady, and he had them playing at atrocious tempos and volumes. Soon the sound became more dissonant than that of a first-year elementary school band.

The cymbalist had heard enough. During a delicate,

soft passage, he suddenly clashed his instruments together with all the force and fury he could muster.

The music stopped. The conductor, highly agitated, looked angrily around the orchestra, demanding, "Who did that? Who *did* that?"

"I've swallowed my harmonica!" shrieked Jones.

"Good thing you don't play banjo," drawled the doctor.

Music teacher: "In the basic choir, there are two male vocal parts. One is the tenor. What is the other?"
Student: "Er—niner?"

An inexperienced cello instructor began his first class nervously. He squawked a few melodies to demonstrate the sound of the instrument then gave a brief lecture about the instrument.

"My own cello," he mentioned proudly, "is an exceptional instrument—quite expensive. Yours are only beginners' models, of course. But in the hands of a practiced musician, any cello will provide many years of rich, sonorous, exquisite music."

One student nudged another and said sadly, "I'm afraid some other practiced musician used up all the rich, sonorous, exquisite music his cello had a long time ago."

NEIGHBORS

"I think the Smiths are suffering from age-related strife," a woman said of her neighbors.

"What do you mean?" asked her husband.

"He won't act his age, and she won't admit hers."

A secret agent was directed to a posh condominium complex to contact an anonymous source. "Williams is the name," he was told by his superior. "Hand him this envelope."

Arriving at the complex, he was confused to find four different Williamses occupying adjacent quarters. He decided to try the second condo. When a gentleman answered his knock, the agent spoke the pass code: "The grape arbor is down."

Looking him over, the man shook his head. "I'm Williams the accountant. You might try Williams the spy. Two doors down."

"I see the Andersons have returned our grill," said the wife happily, glancing out the window. "They've had it for the last six months, and I was afraid now that they're moving, they'd take it with them by mistake."

"You mean that was *our* grill?" screamed her husband,

entering the back door. "I just paid them twenty-five dollars for it at their yard sale!"

The prospective buyer of a home in an exclusive subdivision had to appear before the neighborhood association's screening committee.

"Do you have small children?" was the first question.

"No."

"Outdoor pets?"

"No."

"Do you play any musical instrument at home?"

"No."

"Do you often host personal or business guests who might arrive in more than two vehicles at one time?"

"No." And by now, the prospect had decided the restrictions weren't for him. He held up his hand, rose from his chair, and told the panel, "We may as well call off the deal right now. You need to be aware I sneeze on the average of two or three times a week."

"Dad, I think the Browns next door are angry at us."

"Why is that?"

"They're probably mad because our dog can retrieve the newspaper, and theirs can't."

"How could you possibly know that? We don't even subscribe to the paper."

"Yeah, that's probably got something to do with it, too."

NONSENSE

A man was playing chess with his dog on the backyard picnic table. A neighbor noticed. "Wow, I've never seen a dog play chess before. She must be very smart."

"Hah!" scoffed the dog's opponent. "Not so smart. I've beaten her four out of five games."

A woman in Ireland happened to meet an old friend, who was blind, and asked how she was faring.

"Well," the blind woman said, "I've had to give up me skydivin'."

"Skydivin'! I didn't know ye could do that!"

"Oh, yes. And a fine time I was havin'. But it didn't agree with me dog."

Ron: "Why do matadors wave bright red capes at bulls?"
Rachel: "To make the bulls angry so they'll charge."
Ron: "You mean bulls don't like bright red?"
Rachel: "Oh, bulls don't mind. It's chickens that don't like bright red."
Ron: "So what does that have to do with bullfights?"
Rachel: "A bull really hates being treated like a chicken."

THE OUT-OF-DOORS

The story is told of Daniel Webster who, after a day of hunting, found himself far from home at nightfall. After groping through the darkness awhile, he came upon a farmhouse and knocked repeatedly at the door. It was several minutes before the farmer opened an upstairs window and held a lantern out to see who was down there.

"What do you want?" the farmer asked gruffly.

"I wish to spend the night here," Webster implored.

"Good. Spend the night there." The lantern went out, and the window closed.

Mark: "The scoutmaster says he won't take me along on anymore camping trips."

Sharon: "Why not? What did you do?"

Mark: "I think he's angry because I lost the compass when we waded across the creek."

Sharon: "He's that mad, just because a little compass got lost?"

Mark: "Well, it wasn't just the compass that got lost. We all got lost."

PERSPECTIVE

"Dad, is it true people judge you by the company you keep?"

"I'm afraid so, Son."

"Well, then, if two guys hang out together, and one's good and the other's bad, does that mean people think the good guy is bad and the bad guy is good?"

"Your boyfriend is cute. I love that blond hair and those blue eyes."

"Yeah, he's got a twin, too."

"Really! Can you tell them apart easily?"

"Well, if you look close, you'll notice his sister's a brunette, a little shorter than him."

Marcie has a master's degree in physical science. Each day, she asks, "Why does this work?"

Kevin has a master's degree in mechanical engineering. Each day, he asks, "How does this work?"

Brit has a master's degree in economics. Each day, she asks, "How much does it cost to manufacture this?"

Chuck has a master's degree in chemistry. Each day, he asks, "Could this be hazardous to the environment?"

Alvin has a master's degree in liberal arts. Each day, he asks, "Would you like that cheeseburger with the works?"

A couple and their small child made their way onto a crowded bus. There were no seats vacant, so they all had to stand in the aisle as the bus bounced along the streets.

The child was licking an ice cream cone, trying unsuccessfully to stay ahead of the melting vanilla mess. Sadly, the woman seated nearest the youngster wore an expensive fur coat. More than once, the ice cream brushed against the brownish-black fur.

When the woman finally noticed what was happening, she shrieked, "My coat! It has dreadful, sticky ice cream in it!"

Examining the ice cream cone, the child shrieked, "My ice cream! It's got hair in it!"

PETS

Mother caught little Davie feeding the dog under the table at supper time again. "Davie," she fussed, "you know very well you're not supposed to feed the dog table food!"

"Yes, Ma'am," Davie confessed, hanging his head.

"Don't you understand why we have that rule in our house?"

Davie thought a moment. "I guess it's because if the dog doesn't like the food I hand it, the stuff will end up on the floor and eventually rot."

A notice in a weekly newspaper advertised bulldog puppies. "Cute, already housebroken," the advertiser promised. "Eat most any food you put in front of them. Love children."

The phone rang at two in the morning. Groggily, the man of the house lifted the receiver and heard, "This is 330 Woodvine, next block over. Your dog's been howling for the last thirty minutes, and we can't get to sleep. Shut that animal up!"

Without waiting for a response, the caller hung up the phone.

The next night at 2:00 A.M., the aroused neighbor dialed up 330 Woodvine. When the owner answered, he pleasantly informed him, "We don't own a dog," and hung up.

PROBLEM SOLVING

A little boy from the city was visiting his cousins on the farm. Milking cows particularly fascinated him. "I think I see how you get it going," he told his uncle after watching intently. "But how do you turn it off?"

An elderly gentleman was a hopeless insomniac, and his wife and grown children at length resorted to taking him to a hypnotist. The hypnotist had a remarkable record for being able to cure such ailments—but his services were not cheap. "We'll pay whatever it costs," the mother declared. "Not only is he unable to rest himself, but he's depriving me of my rest, too."

The hypnotist proceeded as expected. He had the patient recline comfortably and then sat before him, slowly waving a gold pocket watch from a chain. He waited a few minutes before speaking at all, simply moving the watch in slow, precise arcs.

"You are becoming very, very drowsy," he began. "Your body is tired. . . . Your mind is tired. . . . Your muscles are weary. . . . You need rest. . . . Complete rest. . . ."

This stage—convincing the patient of his need for rest—lasted awhile before the hypnotist got to the root of the instructions. "And now you must rest. You must sleep.

Your family will take you home and put you into your warm, comfortable bed. You will sleep without waking for exactly eight hours. This you must do every night for a month, at the end of which time you will come back to see me, and we will talk again about rest. . .rest. . .beautiful, peaceful rest."

Softer and softer the hypnotist's voice became. Finally each member of the family sitting around the room was almost asleep. The victim himself had closed his eyes and was beginning to snore.

"You may take him home now," the hypnotist quietly advised, rousing the family. Ecstatic, they wrote a check for even more than the predetermined amount, and the hypnotist left the room.

The sons gently began to lift their father from the chair. Then he opened his eyes, glanced furtively around the room, and asked, "Is that imbecile finally gone?"

PSYCHIATRY

Bridgit: "You look worried."

Brodie: "I am. I'm convinced I'm losing my mind."

Bridgit: "Nonsense! What makes you think so?"

Brodie: "Well, I heard that one person in five suffers from a mental disorder. My four sisters are all normal, so it must be me."

The young, bearded man sat in the psychiatrist's office clapping his hands in a steady but strange cadence: *clap. . . clap-clap. . .clap. . .clap-clap. . . .*

When it came the young man's turn, the psychiatrist immediately asked him the meaning of the hand-clap routine.

"It's a secret ritual," the patient answered. "I learned it from a street musician."

"What's its purpose?"

"It keeps killer sharks away."

"Oh, you won't be bothered by a shark in here," assured the psychiatrist.

"Thanks to me," added the patient.

A psychiatrist prescribed a ninety-dollar bottle of pills and promised it would boost her patient's discernment and intelligence. A month later the patient returned.

"Dr. Strathburn, I believe that medicine you prescribed

is worthless. And I was very disturbed to learn you own stock in the drug company."

"See? You're wiser already."

"Doc, I've been having horrible dreams at night."

"What are they about?"

"Well, last night I dreamed I was in a pasture eating grass with a herd of cows."

"That's odd, but not really problematic. Why does it bother you?"

"When I got up this morning, the corner of my bed was missing."

SCHOOL

Mother: "How are you
   doing in math?"
Child: "I can handle some of the digits."
Mother: "What do you mean?"
Child: "The whole numbers are a bit of a bother, but I
   can figure the zeros correctly every time!"

A fifth grader was having so much trouble with his math homework that he finally had to call in his father for assistance. The next morning, he confidently turned the assignment in to his teacher.

Imagine his amazement when the paper was returned at the end of the day with a grade of 60/F.

"Hey!" the boy cried, rising from his desk. "You've flunked my Dad!"

Teacher: "What do you get when you multiply sixty-three
   times fourteen?"
Albert: "The wrong answer, I'm sure."

The father of a high school senior phoned the Latin teacher and demanded to know why his son had been given a grade of F on the midterm exam.

"Because we're not allowed to give a G," said the teacher.

Biology Teacher: "As you can see from these diagrams, there are thousands of miles of arteries, vessels, and blood veins in the human body."

Student: "I guess that's why old people have 'tired blood.'"

"Mark, can you give us an example of a double negative?" the English teacher asked.

Mark rubbed his chin and slowly shook his head. "I can't think of no double negatives."

Donny came home from school one afternoon and, as required, handed his mother a discipline ticket the teacher had given him.

"Now, Donny, what did you do to get a discipline ticket?"

"I really dunno, Mom. Marv and Ellie were talking to me in science class, and the next thing I knew, I got caught."

A father was reviewing his daughter's report card with disapproval. "You don't seem to be working very hard," he commented.

"I work as hard as anybody else in class," she snapped.

"Well, you teacher doesn't seem very impressed."

"How do you expect us to impress somebody who's earned a master's degree?"

History Teacher: "Why was Washington standing in the bow of the boat as the army crossed the Delaware?"

Student: "Because he knew if he sat down, he'd have to row."

On the first day of school, a freckle-faced lad handed his new teacher a note from his mother. The teacher unsealed the note, read it, looked at the child with a frown, and placed the note inside a desk drawer.

"So what did she write?" the boy asked.

"It's a disclaimer."

"A what?"

"It says, 'The opinions expressed by Leo are not necessarily those of his mother and father.'"

The regularly tardy high school student ran into geometry class a minute after the bell rang, slamming the door behind him. He noisily collapsed into his desk and slammed his book bag to the floor.

"Ken, what kind of behavior is that?" the teacher demanded. "You've distracted everybody. You know you should walk in school, not run."

"But you told me last week I'd be suspended if I walked into your class late one more time."

A fifth grader was ordered to the back of the line for rowdiness while waiting to enter the school lunchroom. A minute later, he resumed his old place.

"What are you trying to do?" asked the teacher monitoring the lunch line. "I sent you to the rear."

"I went, but there's already somebody back there."

"How was your first day of school?" Mother asked Wanda. "Tell me all about it!"

"It was a complete waste of time. I'm dropping out."

"Oh, no! What went wrong?"

"I just don't see any point to it. I still can't read. Can't write. And I'm not allowed to say anything to anybody."

A teacher caught a student chewing gum in class.

"Who gave you the gum?" the teacher asked.

"I don't remember."

"How long have you been chewing it?"

"Not very long."

"Haven't you been caught doing that before?"

"Now and then, I suppose."

"Okay, go stand in the corner."

The student was concerned, because the recess bell was about to ring. "How long do I have to stay here?"

The teacher smiled. "Just for awhile."

"Jim, where's your lunchbox?" the teacher asked.

"Oh, I ain't got none. I'm eating in the cafeteria."

"No, no, Jim. You say, 'I don't have a lunch box. You don't have a lunch box. Sally doesn't have one. We don't have any.'"

Jim looked puzzled. "So what happened to all the lunch boxes?"

SECRETARIES

A legal secretary returned to work after a two-week vacation and sarcastically asked a colleague, "So how'd that hotshot temp work out while I was gone?"

"Pretty bad. He couldn't type more than thirty-five words a minute. Kept pestering us with the simplest questions about using the word processor. Didn't know how to alternate the paper bins in the printer. Made the coffee too strong. Embarrassed the managing partner in front of some of our clients. Oh—and he was one of the worst gossips we've ever had."

"Just as I figured," sneered the veteran triumphantly.

"Yes, it was pretty much as though you hadn't left."

A boss ended the day with instructions to the secretary for tomorrow.

"I've just finished dictating about forty letters; type them up and get them in the mail. You also need to go to the office supply store and take notes on those three new fax/printer models so we can choose one and get the purchase approved right away. Barnes is coming in at two, and she'll want you to go through the new shipping contracts with her—but get her out of here by 3:30 so you can take notes at the staff meeting. Oh, Wilkins wants you to have the contact database updated and distributed before the meeting—and please type up my committee report; I'll try to have it dictated by late morning. Martin's computer is on the blink; he needs you to look at it, first thing. And don't forget to show Abercrombie how to key in the title insurance information on the new forms.

"Think you can manage all that?"

"Sure," said the secretary, not batting an eye. "I'll bring my TV set, in case I get bored."

SOLDIERS

A rural mail carrier at
the end of World War II took the news of the armistice to
an isolated mountain family. He thought the good tidings
would bring smiles, but the woman on the porch shook
her head sadly.

"I s'pose it figures," she grumbled.

"What do you mean?" asked the carrier.

"We sent our Jeb off to join the army two months ago."

"Looks like he missed all the fightin'."

"That's what I mean. That boy never could hold a job."

An army unit on training maneuvers hacked through
heavy underbrush to the edge of a river. "Have you found
a shallow place for us to cross over?" the lieutenant asked
the platoon scout.

"Yes, Sir, about a hundred yards downstream."

The soldiers were exhausted when they made their
way to the crossing point. Wading into the stream, they
soon dropped into a deep hole. The whole platoon floun-
dered in the current and gasped for breath.

"I thought you said this place was shallow!" the officer sputtered.

"Well, Sir, I watched the ducks go all the way across,
and it only came up to the tops of their legs."

The story is told of a Civil War unit on patrol who'd lived on miserable hardtack for days. The soldiers were naturally excited when they spied a chicken on the road ahead of them. One of the privates broke and ran after the chicken.

"Halt!" shouted his lieutenant.

The soldier kept running.

"Halt, I say!" the officer repeated, angered by this display of insubordination.

The private pressed his pursuit of the chicken.

"Halt or I'll shoot!" the lieutenant cried, drawing his pistol.

Just at that moment, the soldier caught the chicken, snapped its neck, and began toting it back toward his comrades. "I'll teach you to halt when the lieutenant orders you to halt!" he chided his newfound meal.

SPORTS

A college crew team had spent the whole afternoon rowing and were near exhaustion. Heading for the locker room, they were stopped by the team captain.

"Fellows, I have some good news and some bad news," he said. "The good news is you're to take a twenty-minute break, and then the college president is coming down here to watch you perform."

The rowers groaned. "So what's the bad news?" one asked sarcastically.

"He's bringing his water skis."

"I like the statistics of your quarterback Evans," a pro scout told a college football coach. "What's your opinion of him personally?"

"Good skills. Sort of a *prima donna*, though."

"How do you mean?"

"Well, let's just say when he makes a big play, he's a big advocate of the idea of taking personal responsibility for the way things happen. When he gets sacked, he's a big advocate of the concept of luck."

TEENAGERS

"When Abraham Lincoln was your age," a man said to his lazy teenage son, "he was chopping wood, plowing, and hunting for food."

"When he was your age," the boy responded, "he was president of the United States."

•

"What's the most difficult age to get a child to sleep regularly?" a new mother asked an older veteran of child rearing.

"About seventeen years."

TRAVEL

A stout businessman took his suitcase from the luggage ramp at the Fresno airport and huffed to the airline's courtesy desk. "What's the meaning of this?" he demanded, showing the agent the large, red-lettered handling tag tied to his suitcase handle. "I'm well aware of my weight problem, but what right does your airline have to comment on it in public?"

The agent read the tag: FAT.

"That," she explained, "is the destination code for this airport."

"I just returned from Germany and had the most wonderful time," bubbled Ginger to her friends.

"I thought before you left, you said you were having trouble with your German," Melody said.

"Oh, I spoke fluently. It was the Germans who had trouble with it."

A man in a tour group thought he had mastered French well enough to speak for himself. With his guide standing by, he approached a couple of Parisians and struck up an eloquent conversation. The locals, however, didn't respond to his questions. At length, the villagers began conversing with each other in low voices.

"I give up," the tourist admitted to the guide. "What are they saying?"

"They're debating whether you were speaking English or German."

The college student was quite nervous on the first afternoon of his summer job as a resort hotel porter. A veteran at the bell desk gave him some friendly advice: "You'll get good tips if you chat with the guests and call them by name."

"Er, how do I find out their names? Do I sneak over to the reception desk before I take them to their room, or just come right out and ask them?"

"No, no. Neither. All you have to do is notice the name and address labels on their suitcases."

With this advice, the student porter escorted a well-dressed, elderly couple to their suite on the fourth floor. Reaching down to clutch a couple of bags, he slyly read the tag dangling off one of the handles.

"So," he ventured, "it's nice having you here, Mr. and Mrs. Leather. What brings you to the islands?"

"How much will it cost me to fly to Dublin?" a man asked an airline ticket agent in Reno, Nevada.

After examining the database for different times and connections, the agent pointed out, "The lowest rates would involve long layovers in Denver and New York."

"Oh, it doesn't matter how long it takes. Just get me the lowest fare."

The agent punched a few more keys and came up with the reply: "Thirteen hundred and forty dollars, one way."

The man rubbed his chin. "That's still rather much, for me. What would it cost if I were to fly to New York and then connect with a train for the run over to Dublin?"

WEATHER

A man was driving home from an
out-of-town trip and called his wife
on the cellular phone. "I'll be home
in about three hours," he observed.
"I see the weather report calls for a
20-percent chance of snow flurries there tonight."

"Well, be more careful than you think," his wife said.
"The children have been building 20-percent snowmen and
having 20-percent snowball fights since lunchtime."

News Anchor: "So what's the chance of rain today?"
Climatologist: "Oh, no worse than 50 percent."
Anchor: "And what's the chance you're wrong?"
Climatologist: "About the same."

After months of discouraging failures in his daily weather
forecasts, a TV climatologist submitted his resignation.

"But you have such a friendly screen presence," the
station manager protested. "Our audiences love you, even
when you get the forecasts wrong."

"Thanks, but I really think I need to be in a different
locale altogether."

"Why?"

"Well, it's obvious that the weather here just doesn't
agree with me."

Skip: "Stupid people are always sure of themselves. Smart people question everything."

Rip: "Are you sure about that?"

When antiques dealers get together, how do they strike up a conversation? Does one of them venture, "What's new?"

Necessity is the mother of invention—even though much of what's invented is hardly necessary.

Abraham Lincoln remarked that common folks are the best in the country. "That is the reason the Lord made so many of them."

Grandmom: "You should pay attention and try to learn from the mistakes of others."

Granddaughter: "Why?"

Grandmom: "Well, nobody's ever lived long enough to make all the mistakes in person."

It's always better to say nothing and have people wonder about your intelligence than to say something stupid and leave them no doubt.

"As your grandpa always said, 'If it ain't broke, don't fix it,'" the father told his son, a college engineering student.

"As my professor always says, 'If it ain't broke, it doesn't have enough features,'" parried the student.

To a kid with a hammer, everything in life is a nail.

Opportunity knocks once. Difficulty never stops knocking.

Wallace: "You sure look glum. What's wrong? I thought you said last week that everything seemed to be coming your way."

Alice: "Yeah. I think I was on a one-way street, headed in the wrong direction."

Jokes and history are the same—they repeat themselves.

THE WORKPLACE

"What do you mean I'm not qualified?" demanded a job applicant. "I have an IQ of 150. I scored 1,480 on the SAT. I was magna cum laude in graduate school."

"Yes," replied the hiring supervisor, "but we don't really require intelligence around here."

Boss: "Why are you always late getting to work?"
Employee: "Well, it's been my experience that it helps make the day go by more quickly."

"What special skills do you have?" a company official asked a job applicant.

"Well, none, actually," admitted the applicant.

"I'm afraid we can't use you, then. We have several unskilled positions, but they're all filled right now by the president's relatives."

The company's management team put their heads together to decide how to reduce the high employee turnover rate.

"They spend their first six or eight weeks learning our system, then they join another company," complained one executive.

"Yes, but doesn't that at least speak highly of our training program?" chirped an optimistic colleague.

A sawmill worker dropped a quarter, bent over to pick it up, and accidentally got an ear cut off by the circular blade. His hollering drew a crowd of coworkers. Together, they started searching the sawdust for his severed ear.

After a minute one of the searchers came up with an ear and handed it to the injured man. He examined it carefully then tossed it away. "That ain't it," he said, resuming his probe. "My ear has a fountain pen behind it."

Boss: "Why are you sitting around loafing?"
Worker: "Sorry. I didn't realize you were here."

A man was complaining to his wife about his job. "They expect us to make every second count," he griped, "but they force us to do things that waste time."

"What kinds of things?"

"Like, we're required to check the bulletin board at least three times a day. I have to walk all the way to the other end of the plant. Takes a full five minutes every trip."

"But aren't the notices important?"

"Well, there was a posting this morning titled: NEW PERSONAL INJURY POLICY. The message said, 'A memo concerning this topic will be forthcoming later today.'"